·Susie Brooks·

Who's in the Picture?

· Susie Brooks ·

Who's in the Picture?

Who will you find?

KINGFISHER

KINGFISHER

First published 2019 by Kingfisher
an imprint of Macmillan Children's Books
6-9 Briset Street, London, EC1M 5NR
Associated companies throughout the world
www.panmacmillan.com

Illustrations: Natalia Moore (Advocate Art)
Design: Laura Hall and Suzanne Cooper
Cover design: Laura Hall
All rights reserved.

ISBN: 978-0-7534-4454-2

Copyright © Macmillan Publishers International Ltd 2019

9 8 7 6 5 4 3 2 1
1TR/0619/WKT/UG/128MA

A catalogue record of this book is available
from the British Library.

Printed in China

For Minna, with love
S. B.

Contents

Who's in the picture, having a **party** at the **palace?**

It's a duke and his friends – they're ready for a grand FEAST!

The duke is wearing blue with a gold collar. **Can you find him?**

January, from *Les Très Riches Heures du Duc de Berry* by the Limbourg brothers (about 1412)

6

This picture is nearly the same size in real life. Imagine painting all the tiny details! It was made as part of a book for a very rich duke, who is sitting at the table. The title *January* suggests it is a New Year feast.

Can you spot...

- a man drinking from a saucer
- **3** yellow and black flags
- **2** green stockings
- **2** dogs on the table

Each picture in this book has a story to tell or lots of different things to spot. So you'll need to use your eyes *and* your imagination!

You might find little surprises, or get a feeling from the colours or faces. One thing is certain – the more you look, the more you will see...

I wonder if it's his birthday!

You can find the answers at the back of the book!

Tiger in a Tropical Storm by Henri Rousseau (1891)

Who's in the
jungle,
prowling through a storm?

The lightning is FLASHING
and the rain is LASHING!

ROAR!
A stripy tiger leaps
through the swishing leaves.
**Is he chasing something?
Who do you think
he has seen?**

Perhaps
it's a snake!
Or m-m-ME?

Rousseau painted this picture from his
imagination. He said his tiger was hunting
explorers! Rousseau lived in France and
never went to a jungle, but he might have
seen a tiger in a zoo.

Who's **skating** on the river on an **icy** winter's day?

The boats are **stuck**, but this is a **FUN** place to play!

Can you spot...
- a lady wearing a mask
- a man lacing his boot
- a hockey stick
- a hole in the ice

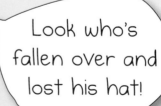

Look who's fallen over and lost his hat!

Winter Scene on a Frozen Canal by Hendrick Avercamp (about 1620)

Would **you** dress like this to go skating?

Avercamp lived in the Netherlands at a time when winters were very cold. He loved skating on frozen rivers as a child. His paintings are packed with stories of people working and playing on the ice.

Who's in the **armchair,** slumped and **sleepy?**

It's a **grown-up** room, but there are **NO** grown-ups **here!**

Ssssh!

A girl and her dog have flopped down on the fancy furniture.

How do you think they are feeling?

Why are they here on their own?

I think she's been naughty!

She looks bored...

Mary Cassatt

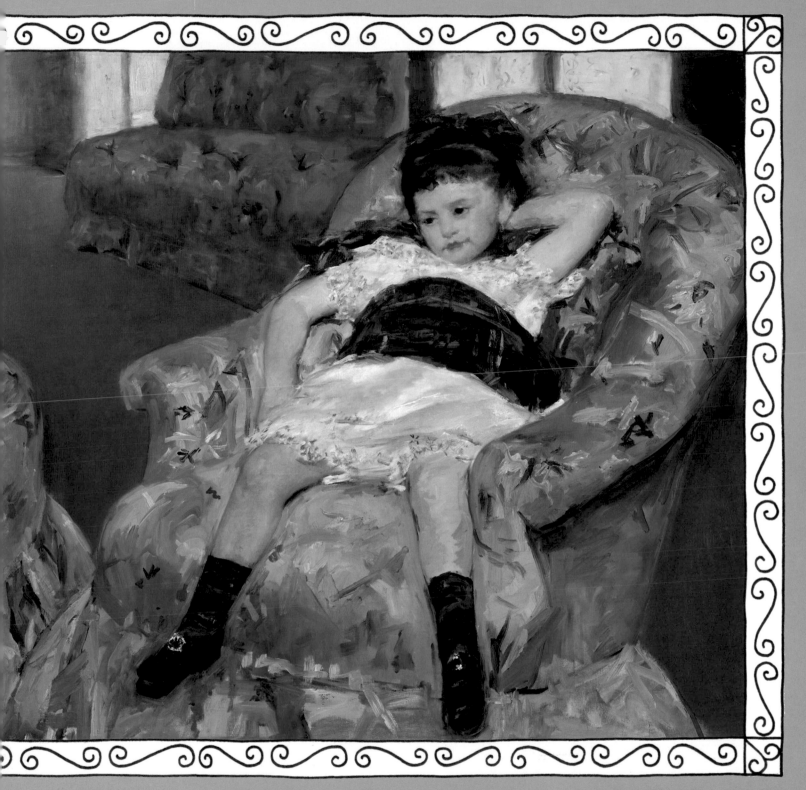

Little Girl in a Blue Armchair by Mary Cassatt (1878)

This picture looks as if it was painted quickly, the moment the girl fell into the chair. Cassatt used swishing brushstrokes and the colour blue to create a moody, fidgety feeling!

Who's crossing the river on elephants and boats?

They're on their way to rescue a PRINCE!

Can you spot...
- **3** swimmers
- **9** elephants
- **11** oars

Look at all the flowers in the water!

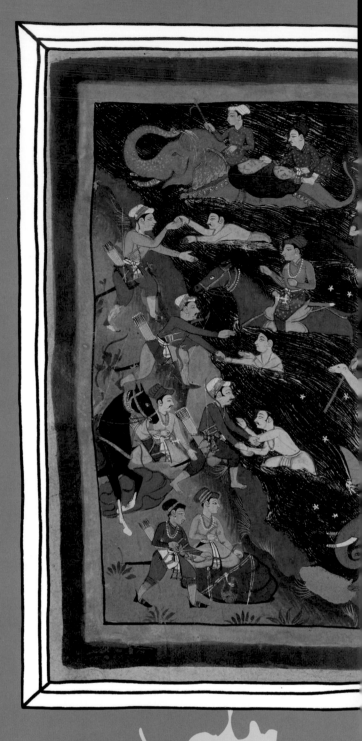

Find a hat in each of these colours: **red, orange, purple, green and yellow.**

Bharata Seeks Rama, Mewar Ramayana by various Indian artists (1649–53)

This is an illustration from an Indian story called the *Ramayana*. Prince Rama has been sent away from his kingdom, and his brothers (in the big red boat) are taking an army to rescue him.

15

The Cheat with the Ace of Diamonds by Georges de La Tour (about 1635)

Can you work out the story? The boy has no idea that the man is hiding cards behind his back — but the ladies know. We can tell from their glances that they're part of the plan to cheat — and win the boy's money!

Who's at the table, playing a game of cards?

There are **piles** of **GOLD COINS** to be won!

The boy with a feathered hat looks quietly down at his hand. **Will he be the winner? Or is someone cheating?**

Those two ladies look suspicious!

We can tell the **boy** is wealthy from his smart clothes!

Who's on the **farm**, parading in the **sunshine?**

It's a herd of **prize-winning** animals – they look so **TIDY** and clean!

Can you spot...

- **1** black-and-white cow
- **1** sheep with curly horns
- **2** horses pulling a plough
- **10** men in hats

I spy two cows lying down!

Summer view of the Farm v.Stock of *JAMES C. CORNELL* of Northampton Bucks county Pennsylvania. That took the Premium in the Agricultural society october the 12, 1848. Painted by E.Hicks in the 69th year of his age.

The Cornell Farm by Edward Hicks (1848)

When Hicks first became an artist, he painted signs and household objects — which may explain his neat, decorative style! This picture has lots of close-up detail, but the distant fields are blurred so they look far away.

Can you see any **baby** animals?

Who's wearing a **necklace**, made of **tangled thorns?**

There's a **monkey** and a **black panther** on her **SHOULDERS!**

OUCH! Little drops of blood drip from scratches on her neck.

How would you describe the woman in this picture?

Calm   Patient

Hopeful   Thoughtful

Lonely   **Strong**   **Sad**

Beautiful

Trapped   Still

Hurting

Serious   Lost

Brave

This is a picture of the artist herself! It's known as a self-portrait. Kahlo often painted herself looking sad because she suffered a lot of pain in her life. But she also loved to celebrate her home country, Mexico.

Who's in the **park** on a bright summer **Sunday?**

People are strolling and sitting and sailing. The scene looks calm and still!

Can you spot...
- a lady fishing
- a man playing music
- a posy of flowers
- a monkey

I can see lots of dots!

A Sunday Afternoon on the Island of La Grande Jatte by Georges Seurat (1884–86)

One umbrella is closed. Can you find **7** open umbrellas?

Seurat painted this whole picture using tiny dots of colour! Instead of mixing paints on a palette, he wanted our eyes to do the mixing. Can you see how the dots blend together?

Under the Wave off Kanagawa by Katsushika Hokusai (about 1830–32)

Hokusai's giant wave makes everything
else look tiny — even the mountain behind!
The scene is scary but beautiful too.
The spray of water looks like falling snow.

24

Who's in a boat on the rough, **roaring sea?**

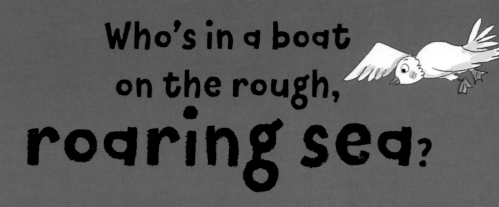

Waves are **CRASHING** and water is **SPLASHING!**

WHOOSH! Three boats **rock** and **roll** about – everyone **clings** on tightly!

What do you think will happen next?

Will the people make it safely ashore?

I feel seasick!

Who's at the stable, visiting a newborn baby?

Crowds of **excited** people are arriving with a **CLIPPETY-CLOP!**

Can you spot...
- **1** cow
- **2** peacocks
- **2** camels
- **3** golden halos

They must be a popular family!

Adoration of the Magi by Fra Angelico and Filippo Lippi (1445)

Can you see these shapes in the scene?
- triangles
- circles
- arches

This colourful picture tells the bible story of the Nativity, soon after baby Jesus was born. The artists painted the three kings and shepherds, with a lively procession of people and animals following behind!

The Dance Class by Edgar Degas (1874)

Who's at the ballet class, leaping and dancing?

Tutus are twirling and sashes are SWISHING!

The dance master watches a ballerina perform, while other girls wait their turn. **Do you think it's quiet or noisy in the room? Who else can you see?**

She looks so graceful!

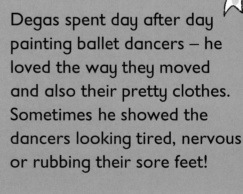

Degas spent day after day painting ballet dancers – he loved the way they moved and also their pretty clothes. Sometimes he showed the dancers looking tired, nervous or rubbing their sore feet!

29

Who's in the kitchen, ready for breakfast?

Two children are waiting for a bowl of **STEAMING-HOT** food!

Imagine you're in this room, sitting at the table.

What can you...
See   Hear
    Smell
Feel
    Taste

That cooker looks hot!

Sunday Morning Breakfast by Horace Pippin (1943)

Pippin loved painting memories from his childhood. There's probably a story behind the lucky horseshoe and the broken plaster on the wall. Do some things in this painting remind you of your home?

July, The Seaside by L.S. Lowry (1943)

Lowry became famous for his paintings of 'matchstick' people, bustling around English towns and beaches. Have you been somewhere like this before? What's the same and what's different?

Who's at the seaside, on a busy sandy beach?

It is **HOLIDAY** time, and families and friends are out to **PLAY!**

Can you spot...
- **4** ladies with prams
- **2** boys lying down
- **1** toddler with a red ball
- **1** girl in a red hat

It doesn't look very warm!

There's a **puppet show** in a stripy theatre. **How would you feel in this crowd?**

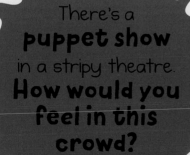

Stables by Franz Marc (1913)

Five horses
are hiding in this jumble
of rainbow colours.
Can you see them?

Imagine them shuffling
about between the
stable walls!

Marc loved painting nature, but not exactly as we see it! He wanted to capture the wonder and energy of animals, and the feelings we have when we are among them.

Who's in the stables, stamping and neighing?

Tails are **SWISHING** and hooves are **CLOMPING!**

Have you ever seen a horse with a **blue tail?**

I feel a bit dizzy!

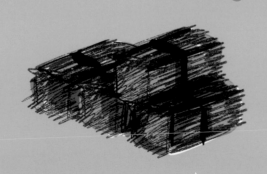

Arcimboldo painted faces made of flowers, animals, trees... even books! He painted a portrait for each of the four seasons. If you were painting faces for autumn, winter and spring, which items would you use?

Summer by Giuseppe Arcimboldo (1573)

Can you spot...
- a pear chin
- an ear of corn
- a peapod mouth
- a cucumber nose

Who's wearing a **hat** made of **fruits** and **vegetables**?

It's the smiling face of **SUMMER**, when all these foods ripen!

Can you see the **artist's name** written in his collar?

Wow!

Try looking at this bowl of vegetables upside down.

The Vegetable Gardener
by Giuseppe Arcimboldo (about 1590)

37

Who's in the garden, dressing for a carnival?

They're up very **early**, before the day gets **too hot!**

Quick! Someone's costume needs finishing – the ladies are sewing it on him! **Do you think the children are excited?**

I love carnivals!

Who is holding a fan?

Dressing for the Carnival by Winslow Homer (1877)

This family is getting ready for a summer festival in the USA. We can tell that the weather is going to be hot! The artist used lots of yellow – a warm and bright colour that reminds us of sunlight.

How many flags can you spot?

The Qianlong Emperor's Southern Inspection Tour, Scroll 6, Entering Suzhou Along the Grand Canal by Xu Yan (1770)

This scene is part of an enormous scroll, which unrolls into a VERY long picture! It shows the people of Suzhou, in southern China, preparing for a visit from the country's emperor.

Can you spot...
- a blue crate
- **2** horses
- **3** boats

Who's in the **city**, parading and **trading**?

Everyone's **hustling** and **bustling**
before the EMPEROR arrives!

This is hard work!

I wonder where the end is?

Who's at the ZOO, looking after a baby giraffe?

They've travelled a LONG way – from Egypt to England!

The giraffe must be **hungry**. **What do you think is in the bowl?**

Can you tell which of the men are the Egyptian Zookeepers?

I hope she's warm enough...

This giraffe was a gift to King George IV nearly 200 years ago. She lived in the grounds at Windsor Castle near London! The cows were brought from Egypt too, to provide milk for the giraffe to drink.

The Nubian Giraffe by Jacques-Laurent Agasse (1827)

The School of Athens by Raphael (1509–11)

Raphael painted himself and two other famous artists in the scene.
Can you find them?

Raphael   Michelangelo   Leonardo da Vinci

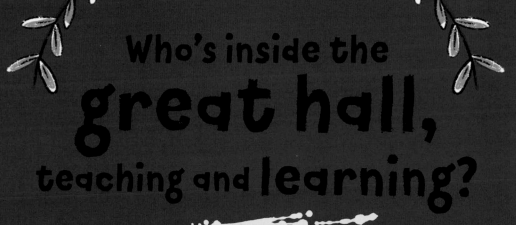

Who's inside the great hall, teaching and learning?

They are all **CLEVER** people from a long time ago!

Can you spot...
- **4** people writing
- **2** people holding globes
- someone running with books and paper

It looks so realistic!

This picture is a fresco, which means Raphael painted it straight onto wet plaster on a wall. He disguised his rival artists, Leonardo and Michelangelo, as important thinkers from Ancient Greece!

Art gallery

You can find out more here about the paintings in this book, and in which country you can see the original work of art. The yellow circles reveal the answers.

Limbourg Brothers (Dutch)
January, from *Les Très Riches Heures du Duc de Berry* (about 1412)
ink on vellum, 22.5 x 13.6 cm
Condé Museum, Chantilly, France
Before the printing press was invented, books like this were painted by hand!

Henri Rousseau (French)
Tiger in a Tropical Storm (1891)
ink, colour and gold on paper, 18 x 34 cm
National Gallery, London, UK
Rousseau discovered exotic jungle plants at the botanical gardens in Paris.

Hendrick Avercamp (Dutch)
Winter Scene on a Frozen Canal (about 1620)
oil on wood, 65.4 x 36.8 cm
Los Angeles County Museum of Art, USA
Avercamp couldn't hear or speak, but he had an amazing eye for detail!

Mary Cassatt (American)
Little Girl in a Blue Armchair (1878)
oil on canvas, 89.5 x 129.8 cm
National Gallery of Art, Washington DC, USA
Cassatt was a great friend of Degas (see page 28). Their painting style is known as Impressionism.

Indian artists
Bharata Seeks Rama, Mewar Ramayana (1649–53)
oil on canvas, 23 x 39.5 cm
British Library, London, England, plus various collections in India
The *Mewar Ramayana* contains more than 400 paintings. No wonder it took teams of artists five years to complete.

Georges de La Tour (French)
The Cheat with the Ace of Diamonds (about 1635)
oil on canvas, 106 x 146 cm
Louvre Museum, Paris, France
La Tour loved painting faces and costumes lit up against a dark background.

Edward Hicks (American)
The Cornell Farm (1848)
oil on canvas, 93.3 x 124.4 cm
National Gallery of Art, Washington DC, USA
Hicks grew up on a farm. He was a church minister before he became an artist!

Frida Kahlo (Mexican)
Self-Portrait with Thorn Necklace and Hummingbird (1940)
oil on canvas, 47 x 61.25 cm
Harry Ransom Center, Austin, Texas, USA
Kahlo taught herself to paint after being badly injured in a bus accident at the age of 18.

Georges Seurat (French)
A Sunday Afternoon on the Island of La Grande Jatte (1884–86)
oil on canvas, 207.5 x 308.1 cm
Art Institute of Chicago, USA
Seurat's dotty style of painting became known as Pointillism.

Katsushika Hokusai (Japanese)
Under the Wave off Kanagawa (about 1830–32)
woodblock print, ink on paper, 25.7 x 37.9 cm
Metropolitan Museum of Art, New York, USA
Hokusai loved creating different views of Japan's famous volcano, Mount Fuji.

Fra Angelico and Filippo Lippi (Italian)
Adoration of the Magi (1445)
tempera on wood, 137.3 cm diameter
National Gallery of Art, Washington DC, USA
A round painting like this is called a tondo!

Edgar Degas (French)
The Dance Class (1874)
oil on canvas, 83.5 x 77.2 cm
Metropolitan Museum of Art, New York, USA
Degas often sketched the dancers backstage at the Paris Opéra.

Horace Pippin (American)
Sunday Morning Breakfast (1943)
oil on fabric, 40.6 x 50.8 cm
Saint Louis Art Museum, USA
Pippin took up art to strengthen his right arm, which he injured during the fighting in World War I.

L.S. Lowry (English)
July, The Seaside (1943)
oil on canvas, 66.7 x 92.7 cm
Arts Council Collection, London, UK
Lowry used thick paint and only six colours!

Franz Marc (German)
Stables (1913)
oil on canvas, 73.6 x 157.5 cm
Guggenheim Museum, New York, USA
Marc linked colours to feelings, such as yellow for happiness!

Giuseppe Arcimboldo (Italian)
Summer (1573)
oil on canvas, 67 x 51 cm
Louvre Museum, Paris, France
Arcimboldo worked for Holy Emperor Maximilian II, whose portrait he painted in fruit too!

Giuseppe Arcimboldo (Italian)
The Vegetable Gardener (about 1590)
oil on wood, 35 x 24 cm
Museo Civico Ala Ponzone, Cremona, Italy
Upside down, this reversible picture looks like a bearded face!

Winslow Homer (American)
Dressing for the Carnival (1877)
oil on canvas, 50.8 x 76.2 cm
Metropolitan Museum of Art, New York, USA
The man is dressing up as a clown called Harlequin.

Xu Yan (Chinese)
The Qianlong Emperor's Southern Inspection Tour, Scroll 6 (detail), *Entering Suzhou Along the Grand Canal* (1770)
ink and colour on silk, 68.8 x 1994 cm
Metropolitan Museum of Art, New York, USA
Chinese hand scrolls unroll from right to left, slowly revealing the story.

Jacques-Laurent Agasse (Swiss)
The Nubian Giraffe (1827)
oil on canvas, 127.3 x 101.7 cm
Royal Collection Trust, UK
Instead of art school, Agasse went to veterinary school to study animal anatomy!

Raphael (Italian)
The School of Athens (1509–11)
fresco, 500 x 770 cm
Vatican City, Italy
The people in this picture lived at different times, but Raphael painted them all under one roof!

Index